Mel Bay Presents

Mandolin Classics

by Ross Cherednik & Ken Eidson

Table of Contents

Classical Mandolin

The mandolin is a string instrument of the lute family, most closely related to the MANDORE (or MANDORA). The mandore is found as early as the 11th Century, having been popular with the "jongleurs" or minstrels of that century and the following two. In the 17th Century, lutes were occasionally made into large mandores, but the usual mandore was about the size of a modern mandolin.

It is highly unlikely that much, if any, music for the mandore was written in conventional notation. Tablature from the 17th Century survives for the mandore; however it remained for the mandolin to assume the legitimacy of having serious pieces composed for it in modern music notation.

Our purpose in offering this book is to fill a gap in publications for the general mandolin public. There exists no single source of the principal works for classical mandolin. The time and money required to accumulate even a modest library is beyond the means of all but the most completely dedicated mandolinists.

We have collected the best known works for classical mandolin and present them in chronological order by composer. In order to include more mandolin music, we have omitted accompaniments. We trust that readers wishing to perform any of the music included in this book will consult the catalogs of international publishing houses, where these works can be found with an assortment of accompaniments.

Notation

All music is written in standard notation in this book. Although historically, tablature has relevance in classical music, it is currently not in use. We have not indicated tremolo, pick directions, fingerings and expression, for two reasons.

1) Scholars are not in agreement as to what is correct for the mandolin in each era;

2) Such things properly belong to the individual, who can then express his individuality through distinctive choices. We include tempo and dynamic indications, as these are commonly accepted. If these words are unfamiliar to you, consult a music dictionary.

Technique

A quick perusal of classical mandolin texts will show a great variety of approaches. For example, some authors demand a stiff wrist for tremolo, whereas others insist that a highly flexible wrist is the key. There seems to be a single area of commonality to all of the authorities: to properly learn good classical technique you should find a qualified teacher. We concur, with the observation that many of the greats do it ''wrong''. Hence, if a technique works well for you, it is probably right for you.

Music

Included in this book are many of the standards of classical mandolin literature. These belong in the repertoire of any serious student of the mandolin.

ANTONIO VIVALDI

Antonio Vivaldi (1678 - 1741) was born in Venice, Italy. His compositions are known for originality and form and are very listenable. He is known for his concertos for a great variety of instruments, including the mandolin. He also used the mandolin as an obligato instrument in orchestral works. Unpublished pieces by Vivaldi are surfacing regularly, one of which may yield yet another gem for the mandolin.

Concerto in C
for Mandolin and Orchestra

Vivaldi

7

Concerto in G

Vivaldi

II.

III.

JOHANN ADOLPHE HASSE

Johann Hasse (1699 - 1783) was born near Hamburg. He studied in Naples and was a prolific composer of masses, symphonies and concertos. His known works include a concerto for mandolin. Unfortunately, many of his compositions were destroyed by fire during the seige of Dresden in 1760. These undoubtedly contained additional works for mandolin and other plectrum instruments.

Concerto in G

Hasse

W.A. Mozart (1756 - 1791) is among the immortals of music. A prodigy, he traveled widely in his youth, performing for the royalty of Europe. His stay in Italy during his teens most likely introduced him to the mandolin. He included the mandolin in his opera "Don Giovanni" and wrote vocal songs with mandolin accompaniment.

Die Zufriedenheit

Mozart

1. Was
2. So
3. Da

frag ich viel nach Geld und Gut, wenn ich zu - frie - den
man – cher schwimmt im Ü – ber - fluss, hat Haus und Hof und
heisst die Welt ein Jam – mer - tal, und deucht mir doch so

bin. Gibt Gott mir nur ge - sun - des Blut, so
Geld und ist doch im – mer voll Ver - druss und
schön hat Freu - den oh – ne Mass und Zahl lässt

hab' ich fro – hen Sinn und
freut sich nicht der Welt. Je
kei – nen leer aus geh'n: Das

22

V.
sing mit dank – ba – rem Ge – müt mein
mehr er hat, je mehr er will, nie
Kä – fer lein, das Vö – ge – lein darf

V.
Mor – gen und mein A – bend – lied.
schwei – gen sei – ne Kla – gen still.
sich ja auch des Mai – ens freu'n

Mandolin

4. Und uns zu Liebe schmükken ja
   sich Wiese, Berg und Wald
   und Vögel singen fern und nah
   dass alles widerhallt;
   bei Arbeit singt die Lerch 'uns zu,
   die Nachtigall bei süsser Ruh'.

5. Und wenn die gold'ne Sonn' aufgeht,
   und golden und die Welt
   und alles in der Blütte steht
   und Ähren trägt das Feld
   dann denk ich: alle diese Pracht,
   hat Gott zu meiner Lust gemacht.

6. Dann preis' ich Gott und lobe Gott,
   und schweb' in hohem Mut
   und denk es ist ein lieber Gott,
   der meint's mit Menschen gut;
   d'rum will ich immer dankbar sein
   und mich der Güte Gottes freu'n

Komm, Liebe Zither

Mozart

Voice

Mandolin

V.

Komm' lie - be Zi - ther, komm, du
Sag' ihr an mei - ner statt,

M.

V.

Freun - din stil - ler Lie - be, du sollst auch
darf's ihr noch nicht sa - gen, wie ihr so

M.

V.

mei ne Freun - din sein
ganz mein Herz ge hört.

M.

Canzonetta from "Don Giovanni"

Mozart

Deh, vie – ni alla fi – ne – stra, o mio_____ te – so – ro! Deh, vie – ni a con – so – lar il pian – to mi – o! Se ne – ghia me – di

26

M.

D.G. dar qual - che ri - sto - ro, da -

M.

D.G. van - ti a - gli occhi tuoi, mo - rir vo - gli -

M.

D.G. o! Tu

M.

D.G. che Mai la boc - ca dol - ce piu che il

M.

D.G. me - le, tu che il zuc - che - ro por - ti in

mez – zo il co – re!

Non es – ser gio – ja mia,   con

me cru - de – le: la – scia-ti al men ve –

der,   mio   bell' a – mo – re!

JOHANN NEPOMUK HUMMEL

Johann Hummel (1778 - 1837) studied with Mozart for two years. A gifted pianist, he also wrote for orchestra, guitar, mandolin and other solo instruments. He closely associated with guitarists and spent five years collaborating with Mauro Giuliani, who also wrote for guitar and mandolin. Hummel's mandolin orchestrations are similar to another mentor, Antonio Salieri. These influences combined in Hummel to produce mandolin music with a lively spirit and virtuoso technique.

Concerto in G Major
for Mandolin

Hummel

Allegro moderato e grazioso

34

Var. 3

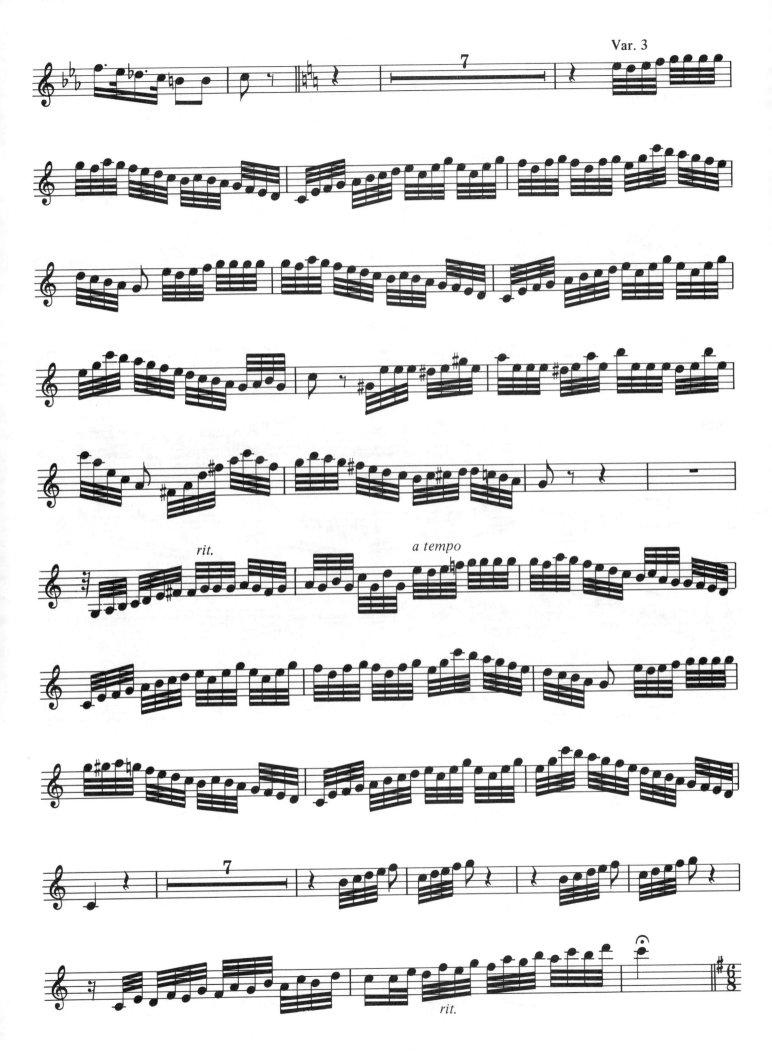

Rondo

Cadenza

Cadenza

molto rit.

a tempo

38

Grand Sonata in C Major

Hummel

Rondo

46

piu lento

p

a tempo

f

47

JOHANN HOFFMAN

Johann Hoffman lived during the early 19th Century. He was primarily known as a guitarist but composed for other instruments as well. His mandolin work includes a Concerto in D Major for mandolin, strings, oboes and horns; four quartets for mandolin, violin, viola and bass; and a serenata in D minor for mandolin and viola.

Concerto in D Major

Johann Hoffmann

50

Adagio

Rondo

56

Cadenza

LUDWIG VON BEETHOVEN

Like Hummel, Ludwig von Beethoven (1770 - 1827) was a student of Antonio Salieri. During his twenties he was closely associated with mandolinists, including Countess Josephine Clary and Wenzel Krumpholz. He composed works for the mandolin for these associates. Beethoven himself owned and played a mandolin.

Sonatina in C Major

Beethoven

Sonatina in C Minor

Beethoven

Adagio ma non troppo in E♭ Major

Beethoven

Variations in D Major

Beethoven

Afterword

We have just examined works for the mandolin spanning a century and a half of great music. Classical music has continuously been composed for the mandolin and is currently being composed. Readers seeking more might start with the vast works of Munier and Calace. In addition, the whole world of classical mandolin duets remains to be explored. Further, a serious student of classical music should begin a study of musical theory. We hope that we have given you a start on a long and pleasurable journey through some of the world's greatest music as played by its most delicate and eloquent spokesperson: the mandolin.